SUCCESS HABITS

A Student's Guide To Succeeding In School, Work & Life

Rockell Bartoli

Dedication

To my family and friends who support me and cheer me on every step of the way. I could not do it without you!

Contents

Introduction to Success!

But Wait!
What Is Success and Do I Even Want It?

I figured before you plunge into this book that we should clear up a few things so that we are all on the same page. I created this book because I want all of the students who read it to enjoy success in **ALL** areas of their life. I have enjoyed success in all areas of my life and I can tell you from personal experience that it has made my life more fulfilling and fun. My goal is to assist you in having that experience as well.

Before I can help you down your path of success I need to make sure that you are fully aware of what success means and what it looks like for you. Everyone's vision of success is not the same. For some people, success is measured by the amount of money they have in their account. Others measure their success by how content they are with their life or by the number of goals they have achieved. What will your life look like when you have reached success? Do you consider yourself successful now? Do you even want to be successful? Crazy that I would even ask that question, right? You would think it is obvious that everyone wants to be successful. Well, the truth is, there are people who are scared of success or can't even imagine what it looks like for them to be success-ful. If you fall under this category I hope to change your perspective. Take a few minutes to create a clear vision of success for yourself and let's put in the work to get it done.

What will your life look like when you have reached success?

_____

_____

_____

_____

_____

Do you consider yourself to be successful now and if you do, how do you know?

_____

_____

_____

_____

_____

_____

_____

_____

_____

Do you want to be successful? Why or why not?

_____

_____

_____

_____

_____

_____

Success Habits:
A Student's Guide to Succeeding in School, Work & Life

Everyone has their own opinion on what it takes to be successful and with so much information floating around, it's kind of hard to decide what you should start doing first. Well, what if I told you there were 35 pretty simple things you could start doing today, like the minute you put down this book, that will directly impact and increase your level of success in **ALL** areas of your life? Would you be willing to give it a shot? If you answered yes, then there are only two things I need you to do as you read this book. You must stay **COMMITTED** and take **CONSISTENT ACTION**.

Are you ready? Awesome! Let's take a look at your current **HABITS**. Not your nail biting, gum popping, going to bed but still playing on your phone for a whole hour before falling asleep habits. I'm talking about the habits you can be seen doing daily, but at the end of the day, they won't bring you any closer to the life you want or the level of success you want to experience in your life. Would you please stand up if you have a habit of gossiping, stressing, doubting yourself, being lazy, always focusing on you, having a negative mindset, or giving up easily. If this doesn't apply to you, then great, this book will still offer you the tools you need for success. If that sounds like you, don't worry, together we can replace those negative habits with habits that are going to position you for success in every area of your life.

The biggest takeaway I want you to receive in digesting this book is that 100% of the habits I share with you can be used to your benefit in your school, career and life. No one wants to achieve success in

school and have a crappy career. No one wants to be on top of their game when it comes to their career but struggling to really build a life outside of work with family and friends. A nice balance of success can be achieved in all areas of your life with some hard work, commitment and belief. So, get ready to challenge yourself and exercise some pretty amazing habits that are really going to open the doors for some awesome things to happen in your life. Once you adopt these habits and implement them in your life, you will eventually work on autopilot and do these things without even thinking about it. Don't forget to bring your commitment and action with you!

P.S. Feel free to start reading any chapter you want. Just be committed to implementing what you learn and make it a daily part of your life.

P.S.S. Why not Instagram it? I would love to hold you accountable and cheer you on. Take a picture of yourself implementing the habit of your choice and tag me @rockellbartoli on Instagram. I'm waiting to see you and be your biggest cheerleader.

Success Habit #1
Develop & Use Positive Coping Skills

"You must learn to let go. Release the stress. You were never in control anyway."
— Steve Maraboli

Are you stressed out right now? Have you ever been under a lot of stress? It could be the challenge of keeping up with schoolwork, sports and other extracurricular activities. It could be the math class that you just can't seem to pass or what about the stress that comes from relationships, or the lack thereof? Let's not forget about the stress from tension between you and your parents about your grades, who you choose to date, paying bills, going to college and everything else that your parents want you to do. Sometimes life at home, in general, can be stressful depending on your circumstances. There will always be factors in your life that cause you to stress out. The best way to deal with this is by making it a **HABIT** of developing and using positive coping skills. This is one of those habits that you will use for your entire life and will directly impact your level of success—guaranteed! How does one go about developing positive coping skills? Everyone has different stress triggers, so we first need to identify them and then explore the various techniques we can use to de-stress, cope, and move on.

What are your stress triggers? Some examples are: school work, arguments, being overwhelmed, conflict, bills, lack of money. What do you currently do when you are stressed?

My stress triggers are:

_____

_____

_____

_____

_____

_____

I currently deal with stress by:

_____

_____

_____

_____

_____

_____

Here are some effective techniques that I challenge you to start using **today** in order to help you develop positive coping skills. I encourage you to try a few and find the ones that work best for you. Be mindful to continue to use them in order to make it a habit.

"I'm stressed and overwhelmed by the amount of school work and other activities I have…. I really can't keep up."

- Use an agenda to keep track of assignments and important dates (I promise this will make a huge difference).

- Use your phone to set reminders so you don't forget important dates.

- Pace yourself and ask for help when it's appropriate.

- Communicate with your teachers and ask for advice when assignments or projects seem overwhelming.

- Sometimes you have to give up one or two things for your own sanity. Identify what activities you can let go of now and possibly revisit later.

"I can't deal with the constant fights with my parents. It's driving me crazy.

- Identify a **GOOD** time to talk with your parents about your concerns. On their day off, after dinner, a time when the mood is calm and they can actually sit down and listen to what you're going to say

- Write a letter. Let your parents know how you're feeling. I'm aware that not all parents are created equally and while it would be great to sit and have a conversation with our parents, some parents will not respond to our concerns in a mild manner. They'll actually make the situation worse and cause you to totally shut down.

- Consider your part, because no one is perfect. Consider your actions that contribute to the arguments you're having with your parent. Is there something you can change or improve? We can't expect our parents to change and improve if we're not willing to do it ourselves.

- Realize that your parents have rules, and you have to follow them. Stay focused on your future goals and know that you won't live with your parents forever; one day you can make your own rules.

Personally, exercising is a huge stress reliever for me. Specifically, CrossFit. When I'm there, I focus on nothing other than the workout of the day and using all of my strength to keep going until the end. When I'm done with my workout, I leave feeling de-stressed and energized. Here are some additional effective coping skills for everyday life stressors:

- Listening to your favorite music
- Exercising (one of my favorites)
- Keeping a daily journal
- Spend time with positive people and friends (my second favorite)
- Do something you enjoy
- Ask for help
- Talk to a counselor
- Volunteer for an organization that you like

Choose two coping skills that you will use today (because you're stressed) or in the future and write how you think it's going to help you.

_____

_____

_____

_____

_____

_____

_____

Success Habit #2
Speak to Yourself Positively

"Evidence is conclusive that your self-talk has a direct bearing on your performance..."
— Zig Ziglar

There have been times when I've been my own worst critic. Actually, on several occasions, I have psyched myself out of an opportunity or challenge because I convinced myself that I just wasn't good enough. I'd convince myself that I wasn't smart enough and the next person could probably do it better than me. Have you ever experienced that? How many times have you said "no" when you really wanted to say "yes"? How many times have you doubted yourself when everyone else believed in you? What could this negative self-talk do to your success? **Kill it!**

Think about some of the negative things you say to yourself and list them below. Don't worry, no one's judging you. We all do it, and I'm just helping you to correct it.

Examples:

- She/He would never date a person like me.
- I'm not smart enough to major in that field.
- I would never get accepted into that college.
- I don't look as beautiful as her.
- No one cares about me.
- I'm not good enough.
- I can never do things right.
- I'm not attractive.
- I don't have any talents.
- I will never accomplish any of my goals.

And go....

_____

_____

_____

_____

_____

_____

_____

_____

Now that you have identified some of your irrational beliefs and negative self-talk, the next step is to challenge those beliefs. Our negative thoughts often make things appear as if they can't be changed or corrected. An example is "I'm not going to be successful in college because I did poorly in high school, so I'm just not going to go." or "I'm such a loser. My siblings have their lives together and I have nothing but a dead-end job." Both of these irrational beliefs have crossed the minds of so many students just like you. But wait, is it actually true? What if your experience in college isn't like high school? It won't be the same because you're going to approach this differently. You'll be going to the tutoring labs when you need help with your academics. You'll create your own schedule so you won't feel overwhelmed. You'll meet like-minded people and create relationships with people who are focused on their future just like you. Get out of your head and go to college; I know you can do it! Maybe you slacked off for a little too long and your siblings seem to have it together, but it's never too late to change. Today is the day because you are going to get your act together and create the life you want to live. Grab your pen and paper. Write the things that you want in life and what it's going to take to get there. Do you need to go to college, vocational school or receive hands on training? Do you want to move into your own place? How much will it cost? Do you have debt you need to pay off? Let's look into that second job so you can chop down that debt faster. Your negative self-talk does not control you, if you don't allow it to.

Challenge your beliefs. Is it really true? If there is any truth to it, how can you improve or change to make it better? *Make a habit of speaking and thinking positively.* You can practice this every day. Make this a part of your daily routine. When you wake up, brush your teeth, wash your face, then look in the mirror and start with an affirmation to get your day started. You say, "I will do great things today!" or "Today, I choose to work with a focused mind". An affirmation is a powerful statement used to affirm that something is true. When you say your affirmation you actually need to believe it. This may take some time but keep plugging away at it every day. Affirmations will help you to change your mindset and realize that many of the negative things you say are absolutely incorrect or simply minor things in your life that just need a little improvement, but instead we turn it into feelings that make us use words like "I can't..." "I will never..." and "I'm not...".

Here is a list of affirmations you can use. Start your day with affirmations. Choose an affirmation that will empower you and compliment your day. Stand in front of your mirror and say it out loud. Sometimes I say mine about 5 times so it can really sink and get my day started.

1. I am a confident, smart and strong (girl, boy, man, woman).
2. I will use my talents to achieve greatness.
3. I am open to receive an abundance of love, comfort and peace today.
4. I possess the qualities required for me to be ultra-successful.
5. My mind and body are ready to conquer the challenge of this day.
6. This day will bring joy, relaxation and ongoing peace.
7. I will achieve everything I put my mind to.
8. I am worth it and I deserve it.
9. I radiate charm, beauty and peace.
10. My life's story will be one of the greatest.
11. I will accomplish whatever I put my mind to.

Success Habit #3
Get to Know Yourself

"When I discover who I am, I'll be free."
— Ralph Ellison, Invisible Man

So, you're probably thinking one of two things. I already know myself well enough or how can you make getting to know yourself an actual habit? I stumbled across this habit when I was in my late twenties. Once I got married and had kids, it really forced me to understand who I was as an individual, wife, and mom. I choose to consistently self-reflect in order to identify areas in my life that require improvement, balance or change. It all boils down to building your self-awareness. Now, you don't need to be married or have kids to reap the benefits of this habit. If you plan on working with other people, having any type of relationship, becoming successful, or becoming an entrepreneur, then this habit is definitely for you.

The more you know about yourself, the clearer your vision for your future will be and you'll spend less time on things and people that don't align with what you are trying to accomplish. Here are some questions that I encourage you to answer honestly. These questions will open you up to yourself. Pay attention to how you feel about your responses, especially the ones that you are uncomfortable about. Is this something that you want to improve? Will this one thing impact your future if you don't start working on it today?

"Me Inventory"

What makes you feel strong?

_____

_____

_____

_____

What are you willing to fight for?

_____

_____

_____

_____

What kind of risks are you willing to take?

_____

_____

_____

_____

_____

_____

How do you feel when your friends or family accomplish their goals?

_____

_____

_____

_____

_____

When do you become jealous?

_____

_____

_____

_____

_____

What inspires you?

_____

_____

_____

_____

_____

How do you apologize when you've done something wrong?

_____

_____

_____

_____

What is one thing you need to improve or change about yourself today?

_____

_____

How do you know that you've done your best and there's nothing else left to do?

_____

_____

_____

_____

What would your family or friends consider you as the go to person for?

_____

_____

How have you bounced back after a disappointment, failure or setback?

_____

_____

_____

_____

_____

How do you make other people feel good about themselves? In what ways do you make people smile? Laugh? Feel comforted, encouraged, or supported?

_____

_____

_____

_____

_____

For which of your personal qualities are you the proudest of?

_____

_____

_____

_____

What don't you like about yourself and why?

_____

_____

_____

_____

_____

_____

What can you do to use your "Best Self" more in your life? In your work? In your relationships with others?

_____

_____

_____

_____

Do you want to improve your level of self-awareness? Why?

_____

_____

_____

_____

Be clear and honest with yourself when completing your "Me Inventory". The more you widen your self-awareness the better your results will be. Review your responses and circle the responses that you're not too proud of. Are you the jealous friend that can't seem to find joy when your friends mention their accomplishments? Do you feel like you have nothing to offer and can't respond to some of the questions because you think you're not good enough? We are not perfect. Go back and take a look at your answers and choose a few to start working on right now. You can become more self-aware in order to grow and enhance your life.

To better ourselves, we must be willing to make an effort to change and improve the specific character traits that are stopping us from being great. Do you find yourself always comparing you to others? Are you always talking about your goals and what you want to do with your life, but you're procrastinating and being lazy? Do you find yourself attracting the wrong type of people in your life?

Daily reflection can expedite this process of **self-awareness**. Ask yourself these simple questions every day and reflect on your response.

1. Is there something I did today that I could have done or handled differently? If so, how could you have done it differently?

2. What did I accomplish today and what am I prepared to accomplish tomorrow?

Success Habit #4
Use Your Resources

"Start where you are. Use what you have. Do what you can."
— Arthur Ashe

Have you ever the heard the saying "Where there is a will, there is a way?" I applied that saying to my life on multiple occasions when my back was against the wall and I felt like there was no answer or solution to my problem. There was that time when I struggled to pass my remedial math class in college, and the time when my mom passed away and I had to care for my younger brothers and help them to cope with the passing of my mom. How did I do it? I searched for and used the resources that I had available to me. I've had to use financial resources, people resources and resources from organizations on various occasions. These resources helped me tremendously with various challenges I was faced with.

Successful people know they don't become successful entirely on their own. Resources play a role in your path to success. There's no need to figure out everything on your own. There's help out there if you're willing to search for and use it. If you're in high school there are resources waiting for you to help with your academics, mental health, college and career planning, family concerns and relationship concerns. Are you using your resources? If you're in college there are resources waiting for you to help you with your finances, academics, social life, career planning, family, and relationship concerns. Are you using your resources?

I've only listed a few of the many ways you can receive help and guidance. If you aren't using them, then you're like a person who is drowning with a floating buoy right next to them. Grab a hold of the help you need and act. List some areas of your life that you might be struggling with (academics, relationships, mental health). If you had some support in these areas things would improve drastically and you would have one less barrier standing in your way of you achieving your goals and doing your thing!

_____

_____

_____

Make it a habit to utilize the resources available to you. Next, identify your current resources, which can also be people resources. These are people you can ask for help like a school counselor, academic advisor, teacher, professor, coach, pastor, mentor, or someone you know that works for a community agency and can assist you with your needs. You also have online resources and it's just a matter of googling your needs along with your location to identify what kind of assistance you can find locally. Often times, there are plenty of non-profit organizations or agencies that can offer assistance or point you in the right direction to get access to what you need.

Everyone struggles and needs help from time to time. Resources were created for that reason. Don't be afraid or ashamed to get the resources you need to make your situation better. Start searching today!

I HAVE MY RESOURCES

Success Habit #5
Join A Club, Organization, or Sport

"Individual commitment to a group effort – that is what makes a team work, a company work, a society work, a civilization work."
— Vince Lombardi

It can be kind of scary and intimidating to join a team of people you don't know. But if you don't give it a try, then you'll never know how much it could have made a difference for you now and in the future. Getting involved in a school club, organization or team comes with a lot of benefits. First, it allows you to meet new people and you'll probably have something in common if you're joining the same club/team. This is especially great for those of us who struggle to make friends and meet new people. It looks really good on your college application and essay when you can mention that you were an active member of a club, organization, or sports team. Colleges like to see that students are involved with positive things along with their academics.

Your schedule is already busy with school work, homework and sometimes a part-time job. Joining a club or sports team would only add more to your plate, right? Well, this is going to give you amazing practice for balancing your time effectively. This alone can be a huge benefit to you as you transition into college, the Armed Forces or vocational school along with working a full or part-time job. The better you are at balancing your busy schedule the better off you'll be. I promise you that.

There are countless benefits to joining one or more of the clubs offered at your school or college. There's the opportunity to network, make new friends, start your role as a leader, and make a difference in your community. Find a club that offers something you're interested in or try something new. Don't allow fear or laziness to stop you from this amazing opportunity to grow your network of friends, opportunities and great future benefits. Make it a habit starting today to join and be an active member of a club, organization, or school. You won't regret it.

List five school clubs, organizations, or sports teams that you can join this school year and DO IT!

1.

_____

2.

_____

3.

_____

4.

_____

5.

_____

Success Habit #6
Don't Become Distracted By the Negativity

"You will never reach your destination if you stop and throw stones at every dog that barks."
— Winston S. Churchill

When I get on the computer to do something important like an assignment, work on my book or pay my bills, there's something I've learned **not** to do. I don't open additional web browsers. I only open the one I need to get my job done. You see, I can become easily distracted once I open additional web browsers. I tend to go on Facebook, Instagram and check my emails. Before I know it, I've wasted 30 minutes of the hour I should have spent working on my book because I was distracted by other websites. Not all distractions are considered bad but negative distractions not only take your eyes away from what you're trying to accomplish but it brings negativity into your life and that is something you don't need.

What do negative distractions look like? Gossip, bullying, technology, and people can be forms of negative distractions. Keep in mind that you don't have to be the person doing the gossiping or the bullying, but the mere fact that you associate yourself with individuals who participate in these activities, and if they try to pull you into, that makes it a distraction. As great as technology is, I personally have lost precious hours just surfing the internet when I could have been doing something more productive with my time. I am the one who made technology or the internet a negative distraction for myself. Sometimes it's necessary to disconnect so you can connect to what's really important.

I'm pretty sure you've experienced a negative distraction at some point in your life. Some of us might have become so consumed by the distraction and allowed it to impact other areas of our life. This is no longer going to be an issue for us anymore, right? Our goal is to make it a habit not to become easily distracted by the noise of negative distractions. Either you choose to make it a distraction or you don't. The next time you come across a person trying to gossip about other people, make the choice to not entertain the conversation. You might be in a situation where you can't technically walk away but if you choose not to carry on a conversation or add to the conversation, that's just as good as walking away. Choose not to gossip, and choose not to add to the gossip. You may not be the one doing the bullying but watching it happen and adding your two cents without trying to help the person being bullied is just as bad. Choose not to be involved with bullying, and say something that's going to help. If you don't want to be directly involved with actions or words, at least report the bullying to someone that can help. Don't just stand by and let it happen in front of you.

You will encounter some people that ooze negativity from their pores. For one reason or another, they have nothing nice to say and they always find a way to make things worse than it appears. This is not only a distraction, but if you hang around long enough you could become that kind of person too. Today is the day for you to make the decision that you will not allow the negativity to distract you from achieving your goals, and living in greatness.

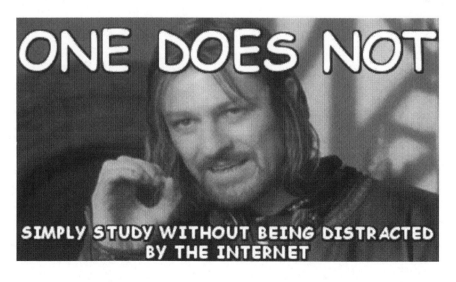

What choices do you need to start making today in order to keep the negative distractions away from you and your future?

_____

_____

_____

_____

_____

Success Habit #7
Give Back and Volunteer Your Time

"You have to sow before you can reap. You have to give before you can get"
— Robert Collier

In case you didn't know, the harsh reality is that it's **NOT** all about you and it's not all about me. At least that's the mentality I have chosen to adopt, because If I didn't, then I could have turned out to be a pretty selfish person. I choose to give back because I know it's going to help someone else. I choose to give back because only a person who chooses to be blind would not see the countless people who are living in poverty, lack an education or have been through some things that are just unimaginable. Make it a habit to feel and care for people other than yourself and the people in your inner circle.

There are endless ways to give back. You can do this financially by identifying an organization or cause that you want to support and providing a financial donation. You can be an ongoing supporter of the organization and contribute as much as your heart desires. If you become aware of someone in need and you have the financial means, be the support that person needs. Fundraising is another terrific way to provide financial support to those organizations that help our community, like the Red Cross and Habitat for Humanity.

Give back with your time by volunteering and making yourself and your talents available to others in need. Volunteering can take as little or as much of your times as you want. Identify whom you want to give your time to; kids, elderly, veterans, international aid, etc. then do a quick google search or ask around to find the organization you want to volunteer your time with. There are a lot of local opportunities so you really don't need to search far to find people in need but it's also great to step outside of our region and travel afar to impact and touch the lives of those who live in different parts of the world.

The funny thing is, even when you're not focusing on yourself and you are giving back to others, you are still receiving something great in return. Volunteering connects you to others which creates new relationships and opportunities to network. It's also good for your mind and body. Giving back reduces stress, combats depression, anxiety, and makes you feel good. Volunteering can advance your career and bring fun and a sense of fulfillment to your life. So, we all benefit when we make it a habit to give back and volunteer our time.

Before you leave this chapter think about WHO you want to serve: children, homeless, veterans, cancer patients etc, then decide HOW you are going to do it either through financial support or volunteering your time and WHEN you plan on starting.

List your thoughts here:

_____

_____

_____

_____

_____

_____

_____

_____

Success Habit #8
Take Advantage of Opportunities

"Opportunity dances with those already on the dance floor."
— H. Jackson Brown, Jr.

Really great opportunities are not going to find you. Those of us who are eager to grow, learn and succeed will seek out opportunities and go for it. I mean, if I knew the benefits of this back when I was in high school, I would have taken advantage of the opportunities to travel when my school had international trips and I would have attended a summer college program while in high school to earn college credits. Opportunities will present themselves at every stage of your life. Let's make it a habit to find them and pursue them until we get them. Think about a few opportunities you would like to have right now. Maybe you want the opportunity to be a leader; to travel, or the chance to volunteer backstage at your favorite musician's concert. These are *real* opportunities. Have you ever thought about seeking them out applying and taking advantage of them?

You see, opportunities come in all shapes and sizes and they fall under various categories. There are opportunities that will connect to college, future career decisions, self-development, growth, relationships, fun, traveling, etc. You don't have to look very far to find some of them. Your school or college has many of the ones I just mentioned. First, you should identify the opportunities you're looking for. Then start by connecting with your school counselor, teacher, academic advisor or professor and they can often times point you in the right direction or provide you with the exact information you're looking for. Some opportunities are a "come one...come all" situation and then there are those opportunities though, that require you to apply by filling out an application in order to show them why you are the best person to choose. You might want to do a little research online if you aren't provided with the information you were looking for. The internet has a wide range of options. Just be cautious and make sure you're dealing with a reputable company or organization. If you are unsure, please go to a trusted source and let them help you decide if it is a trustworthy business or group.

Start looking for and taking advantage of opportunities today. This will help you as you start to make your decisions about what to do after high school, your college major, your future career, and your future goals. In most cases, it will also be an enjoyable experience.

List 6 opportunities you would like to participate in (internship, summer college program, leader of my school club, volunteer for a celebrity event), find them and go for it!

_____

_____

_____

_____

_____

_____

_____

_____

Success Habit #9
Accumulate Experiences...Not Just Things

"I might lose things, but I will never lose the experience."
— Rockell Bartoli

It's nice to have things, right? I mean who doesn't want a nice house, car, clothes, purses, shoes, and everything under the sun? But too many *things* and not enough *experiences* leads to an uneventful life. You just keep accumulating things but little thought has gone into the experiences and memories that you should be creating for yourself, family and friends. Don't get caught up in the things of this life because you can lose them very easily. Your memories and your experiences won't get lost, stolen, broken, given away, sold, or damaged. Make it a habit to experience life. The more experiences, the more pictures, the more memories, the better.

You can practice this habit by creating experiences with your closest friends. Plan a trip, get together for a day at the park, go to the beach, plan a group vacation. Do things with the people you like and care about.

Plan trips to travel the world or visit places local to you that you've never visited before. Yes, it's ok to buy those nice sneakers but remember to wear them on your next family vacation. List some experiences you want to create and who you want to create them with. Imagine what it's actually going to feel like when you step into these experiences. I know that I want my next experience to be a trip to Paris with my family and this is an experience I definitely won't forget.

List some experiences you want to create and who you want to create them with.

_____

_____

_____

_____

_____

_____

_____

_____

_____

_____

Success Habit #10
Do the Right Thing

"There comes a time when one must take a position that is neither safe, nor politic, nor popular, but he must take it because conscience tells him it is right."
– Martin Luther King Jr.

Hopefully, this is a habit that many of us have already adopted, but I know there are some of us who struggle with doing the right thing for various reasons. Why is it so important to do the right thing? Well, because the wrong that you do has a way of catching up with you. It might not be instantly but it will find a way. We are trying to build ourselves up and reach the ultimate level of success in school, our careers and in our lives. We don't need our bad choices to come running us down in the midst of getting that new job, buying your first home, getting married, and experiencing the joys of life.

Do the right thing because it's the right thing to do. When you see a fellow classmate or peer getting bullied and dragged down by others, don't just stand and watch, do the right thing and find a way to help that person even if you do it unanimously. Do the right thing because it's the right thing to do. If you find something of significance that belongs to someone else make an effort to return it back to its owner. Wouldn't you want someone else to do the same thing for you? Do the right thing because it's the right thing to do. Share when there is more than enough and you see others in need. Apologize when you're wrong. It doesn't mean you're weak, it means it's the right thing to do and that's what you're doing. You are going to reap the benefits of doing the right thing even when it's difficult and challenging. Push through and do what is right. Do it every day of your life.

Think about 3 times you should have done the right thing and instead, you did the opposite. List those things and write what you would have done differently now that you have read this chapter.

_____

_____

_____

_____

_____

_____

Success Habit #11
Eat Healthy & Exercise

"Take care of your body. It's the only place you have to live."
— Jim Rohn

This habit can't be stressed enough. I think you already know that if you don't eat healthily and exercise that it could lead to health conditions that have the ability to stop you dead in your tracks. You might be able to get away with it for now, in your very young days but it can catch up to you. We don't need an additional hurdle standing in our way of creating a magnitude of success in all areas of our life. If you are not accustomed to eating healthy and exercising then I encourage you to take baby steps until it becomes a natural part of your life. When we're young, we say to ourselves that we can eat healthy when we're older. We can exercise later in life. "Later in life" comes a lot faster than you think. If you don't implement healthy eating and exercising NOW, before you know it you will be older, heavier, and out of shape. You will have to work 5X harder when you are older than if you start right now and stay healthy while your health is still within your grasp.

There are little things you can start doing today to create the habit of improving and sustaining your health through good diet and exercise. Here are a few simple steps to start your journey. Replace one of your daily drinks (juice, soda, whatever you would normally drink) with a glass of water, take the stairs instead of the elevator a majority of the time. Eat any form of veggies at least once a day, go out for a walk with your friends and ride your bike. Choose a meal of the day and claim it as your "healthy meal of the day" my healthy meal of the day is usually my breakfast. My breakfast consists of healthy food items that still taste yummy. I'll eat egg whites, turkey bacon, orange juice and yogurt or a fruit. Now it's your turn, and don't forget to take baby steps.

What small changes are you committed to making for this to be a habit for the rest of your life? Will you walk for 20 mins a day? Will you drink water today instead of soda? Will you eat a healthy lunch?

List 3 small changes that you are going to practice this week. Double that number each week and keep at it!

_____

_____

_____

_____

_____

_____

Success Habit #12
Set Goals & Celebrate When You Achieve Them

"What you get by achieving your goals is not as important as what you become by achieving your goals.
— Zig Ziglar

Hopefully, by now, someone has shown you the ropes to setting goals and achieving them. If so, have you implemented what you learned? I hope so! If not, you're in luck. Setting goals are pretty easy; actually achieving them requires a little more effort but I know that you're committed and ready to take action. Truth is, if you're not achieving your goals then you're not moving towards the success you desire in your life. It's also very important to celebrate our wins. You worked so hard for it, why not enjoy that moment. It will encourage you to keep going and to continue crushing your goals like a beast!

Go ahead and choose a short-term goal to focus on. Make it a realistic goal that you feel comfortable with and write it below. Be specific about the time you plan to achieve this goal and what you're going to do to reach this goal as well. Also, include any materials you might need if your goal requires it.

I'll start you off with an example:

My short-term goal is to raise my current grade of an "F" in my math class to a "B". Since report cards come out in 4 weeks, I will achieve this goal in 4 weeks. I will do this by not sitting in the back of the class, reviewing my notes before the test, completing all homework assignments and turning in extra credit work.

Now it's your turn!

_____

_____

_____

_____

_____

_____

_____

_____

_____

I fully expect you to achieve this goal. You have a timeline and you know exactly what needs to be done. I encourage you to stay committed until the end; don't give up. Take consistent action every day. There is something you can do every day that is going to propel you two steps closer to conquering your goal. I **BELIEVE** in you. Believe in yourself. Go ahead and tag me on Instagram @rockellbartoli. I want to cheer you on and help you reach the finish line.

Don't forget to celebrate after you have reached your goal. Include anyone who might have supported you through this process. How you celebrate is totally up to you. Go out and have your favorite dessert, stay home and have some of your friends over to have a game night of food and fun. Share your wins with the world via social media (look out for haters! They might have some not so very nice things to say. Just keep scrolling and focus on those that are being positive). Congrats my friend, you did it!

Success Habit #13
Forgive

"When you forgive, you in no way change the past – but you sure do change the future."
— Bernard Meltzer

Have you ever been hurt? Have you been hurt by someone you love or care about? What do we do with those feelings of hurt? The degree of pain someone has put you through can determine how long it takes you to heal and move on. When do you decide to forgive? How do you even start to forgive? Do you really need to forgive? Forgiveness is a habit I contemplated adding to this book but then I realized that some of us will endure more pain than we expect by strangers, family, friends, and peers. Better to be prepared to forgive when we need to than to hold onto hate and pain forever. A habit needs to be implemented with consistency. I hope this habit is one that you won't have to use too many times.

Forgiving allows us to move forward and it relieves us of the bottled-up feelings that we can hold onto. Those feelings that create anger, hate, sadness, and sometimes revenge. If those feelings are not dealt with, it has the ability to grow and impact our health, level of stress and how we choose to handle conflict with other people in our lives. Who do you need to forgive? Your forgiveness is not an effort to make that person feel better. This is all about you. Decide who you need to forgive. If it's possible, be courageous and have a conversation with that person or identify a way to let that person know how they may have hurt you. Their response might not be the one you're looking for but the goal is for them to know what they have done. Forgiveness doesn't happen overnight. It's a choice we make to release the pain or wrongdoing that has been done to us and it gives us permission to move forward with our lives. We choose not to be tied down by pain, we choose to release it and live our lives. Seeking counseling will also support you in the process of forgiving. Please consider this if you are struggling with this habit on your own.

Let's start putting this into action. List the name or names of people that you have not yet forgiven. Write why you have not forgiven them and how that makes you feel.

_____

_____

_____

_____

_____

_____

_____

_____

_____

_____

Success Habit #14
Never Stop Learning

"Never stop learning because life never stops teaching."
— Unknown

Learning goes way beyond your classroom. I know some of you are like "I can't wait to be done with school, no more studying, no more test, no more learning." Truth is, it doesn't end just yet. There is still so much to learn, so many tests you will still have to pass or fail and studying that doesn't come by the way of books. All of this comes with intention and habit. Don't allow life to keep teaching you lessons. Take the initiative by choosing to never stop learning.

Learning can be done by reading, observing, experiencing, and just by having a conversation. Choose the route that's best for you or expand your horizons and choose to learn in multiple ways. Never stop learning means to continue to pursue knowledge and information. It can be related to your career, your personal interest, things that bring you joy, or things that will support the next big steps of your life. Research something you've been thinking about but never took the time to dig a little deeper. You might be surprised by what you uncover. Adopt this habit and it will position you for success in all areas of your life.

Don't become complacent with what you know now. People who excel and grow know that they must continue to seek information, and apply what they learn to see change and progress. So how are you going to make this a habit while you're in school? Choose to learn outside of your classroom. Choose something new to discover or experience. Read more into something you already know just to expand your understanding. Watch videos, read books, have conversations, travel, and explore. **Never. Stop. Learning**.

Success Habit #15
Know Where to Find Your Motivation & Use It

"People often say that motivation doesn't last. Well, neither does bathing – that's why we recommend it daily."
— Zig Ziglar

As a person who truly enjoys motivating and encouraging others, I sometimes need to be encouraged myself. Motivation and encouragement comes in many forms for me. Sometimes it's a simple conversation on the phone with my business coach or a really good friend. I can find my motivation in a motivational YouTube video. I can find motivation and encouragement when I look at my children and I'm reminded of why I need to keep pushing forward, and working hard when I don't feel like it. We all need a little boost from time to time.

Where do you find motivation and encouragement when you need it? Do you actually use it? It's not always easy to motivate ourselves and push ourselves into action. Make it a habit to have different sources of inspiration and practice using it when you feel unmotivated, lazy, discouraged, or confused about your next step. Once you have your list of sources that you can use for motivation, inspiration, and encouragement, then you practice using them. You first need to recognize when you're acting out of that place of laziness, discouragement, and demotivation. You know the feeling, right? It's not your typical occasional "lazy day". It's those times when you just don't feel like completing the big project, exercising, studying, and completing something you started. It's in those moments when you would much rather just give up on the task in front of you. Not sure where to find your quick picker upper? I'll share a few sources that you can start using when you're feeling unmotivated.

1. YouTube inspirational videos

2. Professional speakers that specifically focus on motivation, like Les Brown, Nicholas James Vujicic, Tony Robbins or Zig Ziglar

3. Your role models

4. Spiritual inspiration

5. Prayer

6. Your very own vision board

7. People trying to achieve the same goals as you are

8. Your own goals

9. Your family

10. Books

Success Habit #16
Manage Your Social Media

"Social media is not the place to air your dirty laundry."
— Rockell Bartoli

Social media is great! Except when it breaks up happy homes, leaks confidential information, destroys friendships, allows others to "speak their mind", which really means I'm going to say whatever I want and I don't care if I hurt anyone. The majority of us use social media every day. We connect with our family and friends, we help videos to go viral, we send birthday shout outs and encourage others when great things are happening for them. But, like many things in life, there has to be a balance or we can destroy something that was originally created to help us and bring us some form of joy.

Make it a habit to manage your social media and don't allow social media to manage you. This requires us to disconnect and guess what? It's ok and even healthy to disconnect from time to time. If you're the type to sleep with your phone, check your social media profiles the minute you wake up, constantly updating your page and checking every 10 minutes to see who has liked or commented on your post, then this is really for you! But we can all learn from this at the end of the day. Social media is not the best platform to put all of your business on as well. Some things should remain private and only spoken about in your home, with a counselor or with whomever you're having an issue with. Manage your time and your posts wisely. You never know who's looking at your profile and what their intentions are.

Now it's not all bad news for social media. You are young and social media can also be a great tool for you to network, find a job, share your talent, and conduct business. Make it a habit to use social media for the benefits that will propel you towards success and reach your dreams. Keep in mind that colleges will look up your profile, employers will look at your profile and anyone who is considering doing business with you is going to take a look at your profile as well. Allow yourself to stand out in a positive light when you're seen face to face and on social media.

Success Habit #17
Save Your Coins

"A penny saved is a penny earned."
— Benjamin Franklin

So many people, some you may even know, struggle with saving money and debt. You don't want to be a part of that statistic. I was not very smart about my money when I was young and, boy, do I wish I would have had someone teaching me the principles of saving, investing, budgeting and staying away from unnecessary debt! You, my friend, still have time to make smart money decisions. You have time learn about saving, budgeting, investing and credit. Even if you're not earning an official income right now, you can still learn what you need to do with your money before you start making it.

Some things you might want to start thinking about doing if you have not already is opening a checking and savings account and applying for a credit card (with your parent's approval if you're not an adult) to start building your credit. I would also suggest taking a financial literacy course if it's not being offered at your school. You can find these kinds of courses at a local community college or online. I really love what Dave Ramsey and The Budgetnistsa have to offer, so you can google them as well. The best way to save money is to be educated about your money.

You can make a habit of saving your money, starting today. Think of something you might want to buy that you can't afford right now, but if you saved your money for the next 4-6 months, you would be able to afford it. I want you to know what it feels like to save money with a goal and actually achieve it. If you have no source of income, then I totally understand if you can't complete this challenge, but if you receive an allowance from your parents or have a job, then you should be able to jump in. So here we go.

For this challenge, list what you're saving money for and how much it cost?

_____

_____

How much money do you need to save if you're given four months to buy it?

_____

_____

How much money do you need to save if you're given six months to buy it?

_____

_____

How much money can you save this week or this month?

_____

_____

How will you feel if you accomplish this goal of saving money to buy something you saved for?

_____

_____

_____

_____

Success Habit #18
Make Time for You

"Your breathing is your greatest friend. Return to it in all your troubles and you will find comfort and guidance."
— Unknown

In case you have not experienced it yet, life can often get a little crazy, busy, and occasionally overwhelming. Since we know life is going to be a little off the wall from time to time, this is a great reason why we should adopt the habit of "Me Time". It's the one time that you're really allowed to be selfish. It's the one time when you have the opportunity to just focus on you and do something that pleases your mind, body and soul. If you've already adopted this habit, then kudos to you. Keep doing it. You can be your best self when you have consistent time for yourself.

It's pretty simple and you can start small. I encourage you to have "me time" at least once a week. The time frame can be whatever you choose or whatever works for your schedule. I personally like to take anywhere from 2-3 hours for myself every week. It doesn't always work out like that if it's an extra busy week, but I do find time for me. When I have my solid two to three hours to myself I enjoy shopping, getting a massage, eating out, listening to music, and reading. I get to do these things by myself and I'm totally ok with it. This gives me time to rejuvenate and prepare myself for the next week. Do you have "me time"? If you do, please list some of the things you do during your free time below. If you are ready to adopt this habit. I promise you won't regret it! Write how much free time you are going to start taking and what things you plan on doing during your free time. Remember this is your time so do something that makes you feel good. Some of us love listening to music with no disturbance, drawing, walking, shopping, watching tv, painting, or playing an instrument.

List a few things and start implementing them this week and every week after that. Your future self is going to thank you for this.

Write how much free time you are going to start taking and what things you plan on doing during your free time.

_____

_____

_____

_____

_____

_____

Success Habit #19
Take Care of Your Mental Health

"Don't fake being okay. You only hurt yourself. Be real with what you're going through. Just don't let it consume you."
— Unknown

According to the Anxiety and Depression Association of America, anxiety disorders are the most common mental illness in the U.S., affecting 40 million adults in the United States. Major depressive disorder affects more than 15 million American adults. With these types of numbers, we should all be cautious and not wait to seek help and guidance. When we see that our mental health is changing and things just aren't the same it's a signal to get help immediately. This can happen at any stage of our life so we'll work on making it a habit to pay attention to our mental health and being proactive in caring for ourselves. The sooner you get help the sooner you can manage and cope with whatever you may be going through.

There seems to be a stigma associated with mental health like something is wrong with me if I'm depressed or have a mental health concern. That is absolutely not true. Don't listen to other people or society. Nothing is WRONG with you; it's time for you to take care of yourself and get better. Talk to your parents, school counselor, coach, or pastor. Find a trusted adult that you can confide in. This adult should point you in the right direction. Some of us might require counseling, some of us might require medication. The goal is to take care of our mental health, not ignore it and allow it to ruin or run our lives. We have goals to achieve and dreams to turn into realities. Our mind must be in the right place in order for us to achieve this. You are not alone, you are never alone. You must speak up to get the help and care you need. Don't be afraid, you won't regret it.

If you're reading this chapter and you know that your depression, or sadness has led you to thoughts of harming yourself, then put this book down now and tell a trusted adult or call The National Suicide Hotline 1-800-273-8255-. You are not alone.

Success Habit #20
End Toxic Relationships

"Toxic people attach themselves like cinder blocks tied to your ankles, and then invite you for a swim in their poisoned waters."
— John Mark Green

What does a toxic relationship look like? What does a toxic relationship feel like? A toxic relationship consists of people who are always negative, people who can rarely see the bright side of things, people who are always judgmental and always seem to find negative things to say about people. These people can sometimes be seen as verbally, physically and mentally abusive. People in toxic relationships cause harm and damage. They don't apologize and when they do, it doesn't count because they go back and do the same thing they just apologized for. When you're in a toxic relationship with someone who is negative, you can feel drained, sad, and unmotivated. You'll find yourself not wanting to be around them because all they do is judge, nag, act self-centered, and bring very little to the table.

I strongly encourage you to stay away from these types of relationships and start the process of ending it if you're currently in one. Adopt this habit to evaluate all of your relationships, especially the ones in which you spend a great deal of time in. If you feel that this person is negative, you've addressed him or her about it and you see no change, then this is your signal to exit. I know it's not always easy but this can directly impact your level of success in life. If your boyfriend or girlfriend is always negatively criticizing your dreams and ideas, how is that going to make you feel? If your friend can never uplift you and encourage you when you need it most, then where is the value in that relationship? I know that I can share my disappointments and fears with my few friends, and they will encourage me with their words and actions. That's exactly what you need. The right people in your corner.

Your relationships will change as you grow, go to college, intern, volunteer, start your new career, get married, have a family, and grow old. Find time at every stage of your life to evaluate all of your relationships. Communicate your concerns with that individual who might be contributing to a toxic relationship and give him or her the opportunity to change or improve. There is also space for you to evaluate how you show up in your relationships as well. We want to always be mindful of ourselves. Are we the ones being negative, judgmental, and critical of our friends, family, and significant others? If you don't see an improvement or shift in these relationships then I encourage you to step away from the relationship, or place some distance in between you and that person until things improve. Nothing will ever be perfect but we can choose who we allow in our life. Make it a habit to choose people who care, love, laugh, smile, and encourage!

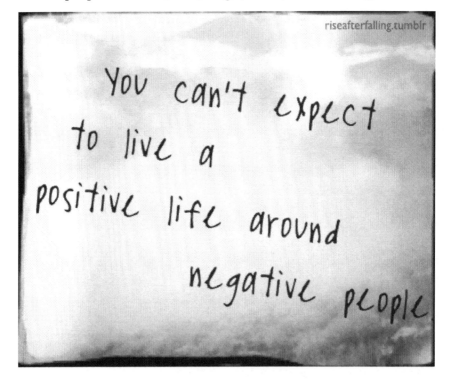

Success Habit #21
Use Your Emotional Intelligence

"Your intellect may be confused, but your emotions will never lie to you.
— Roger Ebert

According to pyschologytoday.com, "Emotional intelligence is the ability to identify and manage your own emotions and the emotions of others." It is generally said to include three skills: emotional awareness; the ability to harness emotions and apply them to tasks like thinking and problem solving; and the ability to manage emotions, which includes regulating your own emotions and cheering up or calming down other people. The big hype is no longer about our IQ and how smart you are, it's about your EQ and how well you're able to manage your emotions? Are you able to tap into the emotions of others to build relationships and effectively handle conflict? Any employer would love a smart and talented employee, but if you are not able to handle your emotions and use them effectively, then that could be a major problem for you and the future of your career. Talentssmart. com says that "Your emotional intelligence is the foundation for a host of critical skills"—it impacts most everything you say and do each day."

Our goal is to improve and use our emotional intelligence in order to help us in our school, career and life. I highly encourage you to read deeper into the idea around emotional intelligence and to take a free emotional intelligence test online. One that I like can be found at (https://www.psychologytoday.com/tests/iq/emotional-intelligence-test). These are the first steps into adopting this habit. We need to learn more about our individual EQ and how to effectively use it. This habit does require a little more reading and research outside of this book, and I know those of you who are eager to manifest success in all areas of your life will do just that. Once you have done a little more research and completed a free EQ test, then practice using what you've learned about this idea and yourself. Put it into play at school, your job and in your home. Pay attention to how people respond to you and how you manage conflicts when you're working from your emotional intelligence.

Do you use your emotional intelligence? Why or Why not?

_____

_____

_____

_____

_____

_____

Success Habit #22
Step Outside of Your Comfort Zone

"Life always begins with one step outside of your comfort zone."
— Shannon L. Alder

Truth is I don't like dancing in front of other people because, well, I can't dance. I was teased so much about my inability to dance when I was younger that I just believed it to be true. "You dance like you have two left feet!" "Girl, you can't dance!" are some of the comments that were thrown my way. The unfortunate truth is when you're young, comments like these can stick and make you feel uncomfortable and decreases your confidence. One of my uncomfortable zones is the zone of dancing. So, what is a girl supposed to do when your family is from the islands and dancing is supposed to run through your veins? My mom can dance, my sisters can dance, so what happened to me?

If one of my friends or family members mentioned going out, I would cringe if dancing was involved and try to avoid those events. But I became tired of missing out on the fun because I was scared to step out of my comfort zone. Eventually, I decided to challenge myself and just go to the events that would require me to dance. The funny thing is, the more I stepped out of my comfort zone, the easier it became. I would get on the dance floor and feel a little nervous. I would start, and still do, by kind of moving from side to side until one of my favorite songs came on and I would just let go and get loose. I didn't care who saw me or who thought I couldn't dance, because I was so lost in the music and having a good time.

I challenge you to adopt this not so very easy habit. Step outside of your comfort zone and take a risk, my friends. Do the things that make you uncomfortable. I know it's a little scary but the benefits will outweigh your fears. It's ok to feel uncomfortable when you're growing in the process. Step out of your comfort zone the next time you are challenged to.

1. Give a speech in front of a large group

2. Go on a blind date

3. Dance (even when you think you can't)

4. Socialize with people you don't know

5. Get creative

6. Stand up for someone who needs it

7. Workout at the gym

8. Wear a bathing suit to the pool or beach

9. Try a physical activity or sport

10. Just try something totally new

What is something that feels really uncomfortable for you to do right now? Deep down inside you know how much it would benefit you if only you stepped out of your comfort zone? Is it asking that girl or guy out on a date? Is it requesting a raise at work? Could it be the opportunity you have to be a leader? Some people would suggest taking baby steps but I think it gives us too much time to change our mind. If that works for you, then take baby steps. I would encourage you to make up your mind, prepare if you need to, be like Nike and "Just do it!" Are you going to make it a habit of stepping out of your comfort zone? Tell me what you're doing and how you're going to do it. I would love to see you doing it on Instagram so tag me **@rockell-bartoli** if you dare and go!

What is something that feels really uncomfortable for you to do right now? Deep down inside you know how much it would benefit you, if only you stepped out of your comfort zone?

_____

_____

_____

_____

_____

_____

Success Habit #23
Take Care of Yourself

"Self-care is not about self-indulgence, it's about self-preservation."
— Audrey Lorde

A part of me always wonders if my mom's cancer could have been treated effectively if she had taken better care of herself. If she had only gone to the doctors the instant the constant vomiting started and did not cease. If only she didn't take the first doctor's diagnosis as an answer to her symptoms, would she be alive today? I don't know, but I question it and it has also taught me to make it a habit to take care of myself so I can be the best me for myself, my kids, my husband, and students like you.

There are countless reasons that taking care of yourself needs to become a habit. Our goal is to become successful, right? We all want to be successful in school, our careers and life in general. We can't do that if we are not caring for ourselves. If we are not monitoring what we eat, exercising, avoiding unnecessary stress, going to the doctor, going to the dentist, enjoying life, and paying attention to our bodies when things don't seem to be normal, then all our hard work could come to an end. You are an essential component of this journey and without you, all this work means nothing. Loving yourself is another component of taking care of yourself. If you love yourself, then you make every effort to put you first.

If you have not already, make yourself a priority. Some of us might need to have a conversation with our parents about our health insurance and the necessary doctor appointments that need to be made. Let's not wait until something is wrong to visit the doctor. We are going to be proactive in putting ourselves first. What can you start doing today to make your self-care a priority? What changes do you need to make to ensure that you are taking care of yourself?

What can you START doing today to make your self-care a priority?

_____

_____

_____

_____

_____

_____

What changes need to be made to ensure that you are taking care of yourself?

_____

_____

_____

_____

_____

_____

Success Habit #24
Work Hard

"If people knew how hard I had to work to gain my mastery, it would not seem so wonderful at all."
- Michelangelo Buonarroti

You're not technically required to be a hard worker. If you wanted to, (in most cases), you could actually get away with doing only what is required of you as long as you're meeting the basic requirements. Wake up, clock in on time, clock out on time and do whatever you want with the rest of your day or go to school, pass your classes with C's and B's, and exit the building the minute the bell rings. Yes, you could be mediocre and do the bare minimum, but if you've identified what success looks like for you in your life and you are determined to make it a reality, then mediocre and meeting the basic requirements is just not going to cut it. We have to work hard and continue to work hard in order to maintain the lifestyle we desire for school, our career and life in general.

Some of us might already be accustomed to hard work. I encourage you to keep it up. You already know the benefits of hard work. You can see it in your grades, your awards, your scholarships, the smiles on your parents' face, and the way you feel about your accomplishments. Hard work is a great habit and I don't want you to get it confused with being a slave to work with no time for fun or enjoying life. Adopting the habit of hard work means that you give 100% of you in everything you do. Even when you know that you could do the bare minimum and get away with it, you choose to go the extra mile and do a little more. When we make it a habit to be a hard worker it does not go unnoticed. Hard workers get promoted, hard workers become leaders, hard workers solve problems, hard workers show others what it is to go from ordinary to extraordinary. You don't need to be a hard worker for the glory per se, but it will contribute to your success right now and 20 years from now. Could you go the extra mile and study more to get better grades, stay at work 30 minutes later to complete the job, step up and take the leadership role in your group project? Can you make it a habit to be a hard worker?

I believe you can and the great part is you can become a hard worker starting today. You can execute this habit right now by focusing on one area that you want to be extraordinary in and putting in the hard work it takes to develop this habit. What does this look like? It can vary depending on what area of your life you're developing the habit in. If you're a student then developing the habit of being a hard worker means studying more if you know that's an area you struggle with, monitoring your grades, keeping an open line of communication between you and your teachers, taking the lead when necessary in group projects, being involved in school clubs and activities, and stepping up to do things for your teachers and school without being asked. Those are just a few suggestions for those of us who want to develop our habit of being a hard-working student. Even though we are not doing this simply for recognitions, your hard work will be seen. Your teachers, parents and school will recognize the hard work you're putting in. Things get even better when you are chosen by your favorite college, scholarships, summer jobs/programs, and internships because of the hard work that you put in.

It's truly such an amazing feeling to see your hard work pay off. Making it a habit means you can duplicate the experience in other areas of your life and continue to reap the benefits. So first, I must ask you why do you want to become a hard worker? It's important to know this first so you don't lose sight of why you are making this habit. Being a hard worker is not for the faint of heart. You actually have to work hard! What area of your life are you going to implement or improve this habit?

Why do you want to be a hard worker?

_____

_____

_____

_____

What area of your life are you going to implement or improve this habit?

_____

_____

_____

_____

Success Habit #25
Don't Compare Yourself to Others

"Comparison is the death of joy."
— Mark Twain

"If only I looked like her, then more guys would want to talk to me."
"If only I made grades like him, then I would get into a good college."
"If only my family was rich like theirs, then I wouldn't have so many problems." "If only I was strong like him, then I would make it on the football team." "If only I was skinnier like the girl on Instagram, then someone would ask me out." "If only I could afford the latest clothes and sneakers, then I could fit in with the cool kids."

I could go on and on but I feel like you are catching my drift. It's so easy to get trapped into the zone of comparing yourself to others. All you have to do is look at others and see in them what you don't believe to be true about yourself or your situation. Social media also makes it very enticing to compare our lives to other people and make ourselves feel like we are not good enough. "I mean look at how many likes and comments she has. When I post my pictures, only a few people like and comment. I must not be as attractive as her." Look at all the thoughts that can consume our minds just by looking at someone else's social media post. Not to mention, most people only put the parts of their lives that make them look good in the public eye on their social media posts. That girl that looks so pretty in all her pictures had to take that same selfie 15 times before she got the perfect one to post. That couple that you admire every day because of their seemingly endless love for each other, have the same fight about money/sex/kids/insecurities on a regular basis. So, don't fall into the trap of comparing your life to the lives that you see on social media. The majority of the time it is a façade.

Everyone has done it before. We compare ourselves to a friend, enemy, classmate, neighbor, colleague, and social media post. We take what we think is our weakness and compare it to the people around us. This is not very healthy at any stage of our life and one more reason why this habit is one we need to adopt and practice. I won't lie, if you're already used to always comparing yourself to others, then this will be a little bit more of a challenge, but I believe in you and I know you can do it!

Here's how you can go about implementing this habit in your life.

1. Take some time and really identify your strengths, go back to your me inventory if you can't think of anything. When you do identify your strengths, acknowledge yourself for having these strengths.

2. Make a mental effort to stop yourself dead in your tracks when you start to have thoughts comparing yourself to other people.

3. If you're honestly not happy about something in life, then create a game plan to improve it instead of comparing yourself to others. Refocus that negative energy and use it for your own good.

4. Decrease the number of activities that causes you to start comparing yourself. Things like social media, reading magazines and gossiping.

5. Focus on your journey. Where are you going and what are you doing with the next couple years of your life? Stay focused on those goals and what your need to accomplish between now and then.

6. Remember to be grateful for yourself, your imperfections, your strengths, and everything you have. Sometimes a little perspective can remind us that we shouldn't be sitting around crying about not having it like others. I mean really, there are people who have no food to eat and are on their deathbed in the hospital. Perspective reminds us that maybe my problem isn't as deep as I thought it was.

Now take some time to reflect. Who are you comparing yourself to and why are you doing it?

_____

_____

_____

_____

_____

What can you start doing today to change this behavior?

_____

_____

_____

_____

_____

_____

Success Habit #26
Commit and Take Consistent Action

"Unless commitment is made, there are only promises and hopes; but no plans."
— Peter F. Drucker

This habit is probably my favorite and most important habit out of all the habits I talk about in this book. Without this habit my friend, the other 34 habits don't have a chance of becoming your personal habits to position you for success in all areas of your life. We all have to commit and take consistent action after reading each chapter of this book. It just won't work and that's not what I want for you. I know that you deserve the life you have envisioned for yourself but it's going to take arduous work. When you are committed and taking consistent action, you will see results. This means to commit with your mind, spirit, heart, and words. Say it and believe in whatever you're doing. After you have committed with your mind and words, then you MUST take consistent actions. This is when you're putting in the work that needs to be done to make these habits a permanent part of your life. This is the part when you write down your goals and put forth the work to achieve them. This is when you buy something with the money you saved each week. This is when you actively choose to stay away from the negative distractions and remain focused on the important stuff.

Action is going to lead to results. It will not always be easy or comfortable. Keep in mind that there will be obstacles along the way. You are probably going to fail a few times before you succeed. At times you might just want to give up and continue living the same way you have been. But I know you won't because your life and your future are way too important to just give up. You will achieve your vision of success because you are going to stay committed and take consistent action. I believe in you and the people around you will see your commitment and action, then they'll start asking you "HOW DID YOU DO IT?"

Success Habit #27
Have an Attitude of Gratitude

"We can complain because rose bushes have thorns, or rejoice because thorns have roses."
— Alphonse Karr

When things are not going the way you planned or it feels like your world has been turned upside down, it's hard to look at the bright side of things and to remain positive. I get it, I've been there before. I clearly remember when my mother was diagnosed with stomach cancer and two years later, the day she took her last breath. I have never felt so sad and hurt in my life. I felt like a part of me had been broken off. My whole family truly felt the impact of my mom leaving this earth. How was I going to heal from this pain, a pain that I'd never felt before? I definitely leaned on my prayers to God every day and as hard as it was, I had to find my attitude of gratitude. I had to remind myself of things I had to be grateful for even when my heart was broken. I grabbed my pen and journal and started listing all that I had to be grateful for even in the midst of my pain. I experienced an attitude of gratitude because…

- I knew what it was like to have a loving, caring, charismatic mother.
- I had my brothers and sisters to support me during this time.
- I enjoyed her during her last two years of life and captured it on camera.
- I had an opportunity to say goodbye (many people don't get this opportunity).
- I was alive with a beautiful family.
- Each day was another day to heal and love.
- It was a gentle reminder that life is short and tomorrow is not guaranteed.

An attitude of gratitude is an attitude we can practice every single day. I think it's pretty easy to be grateful when things are perfect or going well. The real practice comes when things are not the way we want and expect it to be. I encourage you to adopt the attitude of gratitude. Remind yourself every day of the things in your life that you have to be grateful for, past or present. Remind yourself that even though things may not be going the way that you want, there are still other things in your life that you can be happy about.

What are you grateful for? List some of the things, people, or experiences you have in your life that would remind you to have an attitude of gratitude.

_____

_____

_____

_____

_____

_____

_____

_____

_____

_____

Success Habit #28
Network

"Networking is an essential part of building wealth."
— Armstrong Williams

I believe there is some truth to the saying "It's not *what* you know, it's *who* you know." There have been several opportunities I've had the chance to take advantage of because I was prepared and somebody who knew me, felt like I would be the right candidate for that opportunity. The first few times this happened, I was in a little bit of shock. I was like "Wow, you thought about me out all the people you know?" That was me silently feeling like "Thanks" and "Am I really good enough for this" at the same time. That self-doubt can be a killer if you let it.

Networking means we're going to connect and interact with other people along with exchanging contact information in order to create and build relationships. The key word here is *relationships*. This is an opportunity to authentically be you and allow people to get to know you. I believe it's best to first identify why you are networking. Are you building relationships to assist you with your transition to college? Are you looking for a job or internship opportunity? Are you a budding entrepreneur? There are many opportunities for you to network in different places. Start with your school by networking at college fairs, career fairs, and other events. Seek out events happening in your community that allow students to attend, like community hearings, events hosted by your town's mayor or commissioner, and community events open to the public. Now, don't just show up with empty hands. I would suggest that you have a couple copies of your resume, business plan, business card, or a card that has your contact information on it, depending on what your goal is and who you plan on meeting. Adopt this very useful habit and exercise it when you have an opportunity.

This habit will require us to step out of our comfort zone and start having conversations with people we don't know. We'll have to approach people and start conversations. We'll need to put ourselves out there and present ourselves as we network. Be confident, be you and build the relationships that are going to help you along your journey to success.

Success Habit #29
Nurture Healthy Relationships

"You are my mirror, you are my friend, I will support you until the end."
— Rockell Bartoli

Successful individuals who attain success and continue to be successful often have good people in their lives. It may not be a lot of people, but you can pick out those people who love you, care about you and support you no matter what. Success is like a planted seed that requires several variables to grow and thrive. Healthy relationships are one of those variables that will help your success to grow and expand over all areas of your life. Healthy relationships are those relationships that allow you and the other individual to laugh and cry together, smile, and encourage and show up for each other when it's needed the most. Healthy relationships elevate our success by keeping us focused, on track and redirecting us when we get off track.

The habit I encourage you to practice is nourishing and growing these types of relationships. This can be done by staying in touch, being present, and demonstrating your ability to be positive, loving, and encouraging in your relationships as well. Our responsibility of staying in touch is as simple as making a phone call, sending a text message and even using snail mail from time to time. Don't allow our day to day routine and success to forget about the people who have been there for us. We also need to show up the same way we expect our family and friends to show up when we need them. This is all a two-way street. Being present can mean that you're available to listen to someone else vent over the phone or showing up to birthday parties, get togethers, dinner, lunch, and other important events. I know that we are all busy and we can't attend every event, but the big goal here is to show up when you can and make it count. Make it a habit to mirror the positive, caring, and honest vibes your friends and family are giving to you. Show that you care with your words and actions. Nurture these healthy important relationships so they last a lifetime.

List the people you have a healthy relationship with and the next thing you plan to do for that person to nourish your relationship with them.

Example: My aunt- I will send her a card in the mail for her birthday.

_____

_____

_____

_____

_____

_____

_____

_____

_____

_____

_____

Success Habit #30
Manage Your Time

"Time is the most valuable coin in your life. You and you alone will determine how that coin will be spent. Be careful that you do not let other people spend it for you."
— Carl Sandburg

It took me a little while, but I finally realized that my time was just as valuable as my money. So, the same way I try not to waste my money is the same way I try not to waste my precious time. I didn't always have this mindset. I was a bit of a procrastinator at times and that came back to bite me in the butt when the final product for my assignments and projects would turn out to be less than stellar. Not being able to manage my time would cause me to make excuses and people who frequently make excuses are not on the right path to success. After some much-needed constructive criticism and getting tired of always catching up and forgetting things, I figured that I better start making some changes or things will just remain the same.

This habit is for those of us who struggle to manage our time effectively, and for those of us who can use a few pointers for managing our time and getting more done. Truth is, when we don't manage our time properly, it impacts us in in multiple ways. It will affect the way we feel and how other people perceive us, or how smooth our day runs. Adopting this habit means that we'll have to make a few changes to the way we currently do things. The changes are small but require consistency in order for it to work and become a habit.

I would suggest that you start with buying and using an agenda. It will help you to keep track of your activities, homework and assignments. You must practice using and reviewing your agenda every day.

This is how it becomes a habit. If you prefer, you can also use an on-line calendar (google) and sync it with your phone so that you receive reminders on your phone when things are due or need your attention. Another important part of managing your time is to prioritize the events of your day and tackle the most important things first. When we fail to manage our time, we can feel overwhelmed. Practice balancing your schedule by not putting too much on your plate in one day or week, if it's avoidable. This often means that we can't wait until the last minute to get things done. Learn to manage your time and your day so that you have control. No more running out the house like a crazy person and trying to run people over in traffic because your time management is off. Choose to do better starting today. Here are some additional tips you can use that will help you.

- Take out your clothes for work or school the night before so you don't waste time in the morning trying to figure out what to wear.

- Pack your lunch and snacks the night before.

- Put reminders on your phone to notify you of appointments and important events.

- Create a to do list and use it during the day.

- Set your clock 10 minutes ahead of the original time (it will create a sense of urgency).

- Put your alarm clock away from your bed so you have to get up and get it thus avoid falling back asleep.

What change are you going to implement today to improve the way you manage your time?

_____

_____

_____

_____

_____

_____

Success Habit #31
Constructive Criticism
"To avoid criticism, say nothing, do nothing, be nothing."
— Elbert Hubbard

The old me would become easily discouraged, mad or sad when someone would criticize me. I guess it's because I didn't know what to do with the feedback or observations that were given to me. I kind of threw everything under the same umbrella of "you just don't like me" or "you have a problem with me". That was my defense mechanism to criticism. So, when I got my first job and my employer pulled me to the side to inform me that I wasn't working fast enough and that I needed to pick up my pace, I went a little crazy. I actually cried that night, my feelings were hurt. Here I thought that I was doing an excellent job and my boss thought otherwise. Then all of my irrational thoughts started to flow in. "I know, maybe he doesn't like me and he's probably going to fire me." At the end of the day, he was just trying to tell me to work a little more efficiently and it had nothing to do with him not liking me or wanting to fire me.

Fast forward to today. I actually look forward to constructive criticism because I believe that I am a work in progress and there is always room for improvement. I'm at a point in my life where I can really tell if someone is trying to help me with their words or trying to put me down. This is something that you develop over time and it requires practice. It requires you becoming ok with people giving constructive criticism or criticism in general. To adopt this habit, you first have to recognize that you are doing this because you want to better yourself and grow as an individual. If we are looking to improve ourselves then we must take into consideration the observations and feedback that our peers, friends, family, and colleagues provide us.

The first thing we do when we are given any form of criticism is to verify if the information has any truth to it. If you honestly believe it's not true then you might want to ask the person who's speaking to you to give you some concrete examples of what he or she is talking about specifically. If there are no concrete examples than you can kindly thank that person, if you feel like it, and then move forward with your day, not much to do here right? However, if the feedback is true or the individual is able to provide you with very clear examples then we have a different situation. At this point, we can start to evaluate how this feedback can help us and what needs to be done in order to better the situation or ourselves.

If you're not quite sure what to do then you have a few options. You can either ask the person giving you constructive criticism for examples of how they think you can improve or to make suggestions to whatever you both have discussed. You can also seek the advice of someone in your life that you respect, look up to and cares about you. This could be your parent, coach, counselor, pastor, etc. After you have some tips and tricks in your toolbox then it's all a matter of committing to what needs to be done and taking consistent action. This is how we grow, this is how we never stay the same because we are always finding ways to improve.

Don't look at constructive criticism as anything less than a tool to help us develop and grow. If you stumble across a few people who are just there to criticize, and bring you down then don't associate yourself with them and focus on what you know to be true!

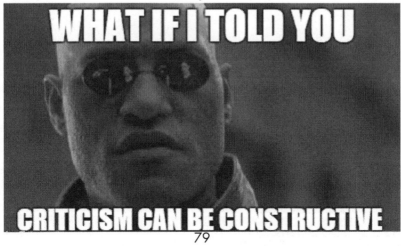

Success Habit #32
Have Fun & Enjoy Life

"When he worked, he really worked. But when he played, he really PLAYED."
— Dr. Seuss

Who would ever think we'd need to make having fun an actual habit? Having fun makes the majority of us feel good so it's probably something we're going to do automatically, right? Well, I know some people right now who aren't having much fun in their lives for various reasons. There's that individual who is caught up in working and making money. Fun is at the bottom of his list of things to do. I also know a young lady who is so consumed with being what everyone else wants her to be, including parents & family, that she forgets to be herself and have fun sometimes. What about all the young adults who forget what it's like to have fun because life has just fully taken over and they don't create a space for fun, laughter and friends in the midst of the chaos of life.

Like everything else in life, we need to have a good balance, or something we view as good and fun can very quickly turn into something bad. I like the saying "work hard, play hard" and I try my best to live my life in alignment with this saying. We're all going to work hard to create the life we want for ourselves and our families, but we can't forget to stop and enjoy life when those opportunities arise. We can also create those opportunities for ourselves. My co-workers and I have created a once-a-month, girls' night out. On this particular night, we choose an event like the movies, painting, mall, dinner, etc. and we make sure to have fun and enjoy each other's company. Life is full of ups and downs and we have a lot of hard work ahead of us if we are determined to create a magnitude of success that flows into all areas of our lives. Just make sure you find time to laugh until your stomach hurts, smile until to your cheeks can't handle it anymore and enjoy your life. You only have one!

What do you currently do to break, have fun, and enjoy life?

_____

_____

_____

_____

_____

If you don't find yourself having fun or enjoying life, why aren't you? Decide today to create a space for fun. Choose to do something this week that brings joy to your life and puts a smile on your face. What will that be?

_____

_____

_____

_____

_____

_____

Success Habit #33
Perspective

"Most misunderstandings in the world could be avoided if people would simply take the time to ask, "What else could this mean?"
-Shannon L. Alder

According to google, the definition of perspective is "a particular attitude towards something or way of regarding something; a point of view." Perspective gives you full control on how you want to view something and can often change the way we feel. It allows you to engage in a mind shift and step outside of the situation so you can have a bird's eye view of what's going on, which leads to better outcomes. Consider perspective as a pair of glasses you put on when you want to change your way of thinking or feeling. Perspective can instantly change your attitude and help you to solve problems. I practice using my perspective especially when I'm not happy about an outcome, I don't agree with something, or I'm being negative. It's those times that I find myself responding based on my feelings and not really looking at the issue at hand. Your attitude towards something can always be changed with good reasoning. It's really our negative attitude that requires the most change and your ability to look at your situation from another angle will give you perspective.

Practice implementing this very valuable habit into your life. Put on your perspective glasses and choose to see that your situation can be viewed differently. Choose to see the positive, choose to find additional ways to solve the problem, choose to see that your struggle is temporary and focus on what you can start doing now to better your situation. You have opportunities right now to practice using your perspective. Think about some of your current struggles, things you're not happy about and events that have not turned out the way you expected. Are you stressed out by any of these things, do you become

Perspective

emotional or are you angry? Have you tried looking at that particular thing from different angles, are there other options, are you being irrational, is it something that's out of your control but you can't seem to let it go? Perspective can help you to change what you think and how you feel.

List three things that you want to change your perspective on and how you plan on doing it.

1._____

_____

2._____

_____

3._____

_____

Success Habit #34
Self-Control

"You have power over your mind – not outside events. Realize this, and you will find strength."
— Marcus Aurelius

It seems pretty easy, right? All you need to do is practice self-control. Yet, every day we see people doing things based off of feelings and a lack of self-control. Self-control should be exercised in all areas of our lives not just when it's convenient or easy. Self-control should be seen on the roads we drive on-not road rage, self-control should be seen on black Friday when patiently waiting in lines, not people beating each other up for material things. You have total control of yourself, correct? So why is it difficult for some of us to display that? We can't grow towards success if we lack self-control. We'll end up wasting our money, losing family and friendships, and struggle to stay on track when we are working towards our goals.

If you adopt the habit of displaying and exercising self-control, then you are on the right track. The best way to start implementing this habit is simply by thinking before you act or respond. Whenever you are asked a question, placed in an awkward position, confronted, accused, or any other situation that may cause you to lose self-control, I highly encourage you to stop, think and breathe before responding. Here are some things to think about before you respond.

"Is this true?"
"How will my response impact my job?"
"How will my actions impact my family?"
"How will people perceive me after my response?"
"What is the best way to respond?"

"Will the way I respond lead to jail time or death?"
"Is it better to just walk away instead of responding?"
"Do I need to calm down before responding?"

Pay attention to your body and the physical signs before you take action in any situation. Do you feel your heart beating, are you breathing heavily, is your body tense, do you feel angry or aggravated? These are some signs that you might be on the verge of losing control. This might be a good time to walk away and cool down.

I also advise you to practice self-control with your finances. Don't become an impulse spender, stay focused on things you need and occasionally buy things you want. Always keep your receipts. You can go home and look at the things you've purchased and ask yourself if you really needed it. If you didn't, then you can take it back to the store with your receipt and get your money back. Practice self-control in your relationships. If you want your significant other being faithful to you, then we must do the same. Self-control means not seeing people outside of your relationship. If you find that you are struggling with displaying self-control, then I would encourage you to speak to a trusted adult who can point you in the right direction to get you the help you need. You can practice self-control in all areas of your life if you commit and take consistent action. Your future success will thank you for it.

List three areas of your life where you need to implement self-control (finances, health, anger, etc.).

1. _____

2. _____

3. _____

What will you start doing to have more self-control in those three areas of your life?

4. _____

5. _____

6. _____

Success Habit #35
Make Your Past Stay in The Past

"The past is never where you think you left it."
— Katherine Anne Porter

I have been guilty of allowing my past to repeatedly pop up in my life and make me second guess myself. For some reason, it was hard for me to let go of it and each time I declared I was over my past mistakes, it would just come creeping back into my mind. I realized that it was paralyzing me and not allowing me to be confident in myself. I took some time to work on this by reading and following the stories of other people who dealt with this. I had to change my thought process and continue to work at it if I was absolutely serious about making my past a part of my past and not allowing it to hinder my present performance or future.

If you want your past to remain there, then this habit is going to require some work as all of these success habits do. Here are some action steps you can start taking to implement this habit into your life.

1. Accept your past as a part of the story in your life and acknowledge that you can't change it, but you can work to make sure that it does not repeat itself.

2. If you need to be healed by the pain of your past then seek counseling, pray, journal, join a support group and identify healthy ways to help you heal. Don't ignore this step!

3. Find power in your past by sharing it with other people who can benefit from hearing your story. This can be healing for you and your audience.

4. Forgive yourself and anyone else who might have been involved. Forgiveness is about allowing you to heal. We can't move forward if we're still crippled in pain.

5. Remember it's your past, stay focused on the YOU right now!

Choose any of these action steps and take it one step at a time. I believe in you.

Conclusion

When It's All Said & Done

"Good habits formed at youth make all the difference."
-Aristotle

I have been gifted with a talent to help young people succeed and become the best person they can be. I accomplish this in my role as a school counselor, professor, professional speaker, and author. I wrote this entire book thinking about you, your future, and your current situation. I thought about the obstacles you're facing now, the ones you'll face in the future and the ones you're not aware of but are right around the corner. I considered the fact that you might doubt yourself and fail to see how truly capable you are of achieving ANYTHING you put your mind and hard work too. Trust me when I say the chapters you've just read have the ability to change your life right now (if you choose to implement them) and the ability to position you for the type of success you have envisioned for your life.

I guess when it's all said and done, your desire for success is going to drive you to make the necessary changes that will lead to you living a successful life. There's no secret formula to success. If you read this book, commit, and take consistent action, then you are positioning yourself to achieve your goals and live out your dreams. These habits are truly important and you can expect to use them forever. That's how you'll experience success in all areas of your life. Believe in yourself and never give up!

Please look me up on Instagram and tag me @rockellbartoli so I can see you in action. I would love the opportunity to cheer you on and virtually meet you.

I believe in YOU! I hope that you believe in YOU too!

Made in the USA
Columbia, SC
05 September 2018